NATURAL SOLUTION FOR OBSESSIVE COMPULSIVE DISORDER

Empower Your Mind: Holistic Strategies For Finding Freedom And Overcoming Neurotic Naturally

DR. JEREMY ALLEY

Disclaimer:

The information provided in this book, is intended for general informational purposes only and should not be considered as professional advice.

The author has made every effort to ensure the accuracy of the information presented. However, readers are advised to consult with a qualified healthcare professional before attempting any herbal remedies or making significant changes to their wellness routine. Individual health conditions vary, and what may be suitable for one person may not be appropriate for another.

It is important to note that the author is not in any endorsement deal, partnership, or affiliation with any organization, brand, or company mentioned in this book. Any references to specific products or services are based on the author's personal experience or general knowledge and do not imply an endorsement or promotion of those products or services.

Contents

First of all,

The mental health illness known as obsessive-compulsive disorder (OCD) is typified by recurrent, bothersome thoughts (called obsessions) and repetitive actions or thoughts (called compulsions). It can have a big effect on a person's relationships, daily life, and general well-being. This investigation explores the possibility of using herbal remedies to manage the difficulties and symptoms related to OCD.

About This Book

It's important to comprehend the intricacies of OCD to appreciate the significance of natural remedies. Driven by an excessive impulse to lessen anxiety or prevent a feared outcome, the illness presents itself in a variety of ways, such as checking, counting, cleaning, or repeating behaviors. These customs have the potential to become laborious and disruptive to day-to-day activities. People of all ages are affected by OCD, and while its precise cause is still unknown, it is thought to be a result of a confluence of environmental, behavioral, neurological, genetic, and cognitive variables.

Medications like selective serotonin reuptake inhibitors (SSRIs) and psychotherapies like cognitive-behavioral therapy (CBT) are common components of traditional OCD treatments. However, people are turning to complementary and alternative medicines, such as herbal remedies, due to the negative effects or low effectiveness of these traditional approaches.

The Value of Herbal Remedies

Herbal remedies are significant for OCD management since they can provide natural, holistic techniques that can be used in conjunction with traditional treatments. While studies on the effectiveness of herbal treatments for OCD are still underway, several herbs have demonstrated promise in treating stress and anxiety, two conditions that are frequently linked to symptoms of obsessive-compulsive disorder.

Herbs with relaxing effects on the nervous system include valerian root, chamomile, and passionflower. These herbs have the potential to be helpful for people with OCD since they may lower anxiety levels. Furthermore, adaptogenic herbs like Rhodiola rosea and ashwagandha may help to balance the body's stress response, which may lead to a more balanced mental state.

Herbal remedies for OCD must be used carefully, taking into account individual variances and seeking advice from medical experts.

To avoid any negative consequences, the interaction between herbs and drugs needs to be closely watched.

Furthermore, the potential advantages of these herbal medicines can be increased by combining them with a thorough treatment plan that includes lifestyle modifications and therapy.

A comprehensive approach to mental health is essential, as demonstrated by our understanding of OCD and investigation of herbal remedies. Herbal therapies are significant because they can serve as natural substitutes for conventional treatments and give people more tools to deal with the difficulties associated with obsessive-compulsive disorders.

CHAPTER ONE

COMPULSIVE-OBSESSIVE DISORDERS: A GUIDE

The mental health illness known as obsessive-compulsive disorder (OCD) is typified by recurrent, bothersome thoughts (called obsessions) and repetitive actions or thoughts (called compulsions). OCD sufferers frequently struggle to regulate these thoughts and behaviors, which causes them great distress. Investigating practical herbal remedies requires an understanding of the nature of OCD.

OCD: What Is It?

People of all ages are affected by the complicated psychiatric illness known as OCD. It consists of a vicious loop of compulsions—repetitive actions or mental rituals carried out to reduce the anxiety brought on by the obsessions—and obsessions—unwanted and upsetting thoughts. A person's everyday life, relationships, and general well-being can all be profoundly impacted by OCD.

Typical Symptoms

Compulsive activities like excessive handwashing, checking, counting, or repeating certain acts are common symptoms of OCD. Other common symptoms include obsessive thinking about cleanliness, order, symmetry, fear of harm to oneself or others, and the need for things to be "just right." It is essential to comprehend these symptoms to choose herbal medicines that work.

Reasons And Initiators

Although the precise etiology of OCD is unknown, several factors, including genetic, neurological, behavioral, cognitive, and environmental ones, may be involved in its development. The beginning or worsening of OCD symptoms can be triggered by trauma, stress, or major life changes. Investigating the underlying causes aids in creating herbal remedies that are specifically tailored to the requirements of OCD sufferers.

Herbal therapies provide a comprehensive strategy for treating obsessive-compulsive disorders, emphasizing anxiety reduction, mental health support, and resolving underlying imbalances. These all-natural remedies can be incorporated into a whole treatment plan or used in conjunction with more conventional therapeutic modalities.

Overview Of Herbal Remedies

For millennia, people have relied on the therapeutic qualities of plants to treat psychological issues. This practice of using herbs for mental health stretches back to many cultures. Plants recognized for their relaxing, anxiety-relieving, and mood-stabilizing properties are frequently used in herbal treatments for OCD. While these treatments might not be a substitute for expert medical guidance, they might be beneficial complements to a comprehensive health program.

Herbal Medicine's Power

The medicinal qualities of plants are tapped into by herbal medicine to enhance both physical and mental health. Numerous herbs have adaptogenic properties that aid in the body's and mind's adjustment to stimuli.

Herbs with soothing and anxiolytic (anxiety-reducing) properties are very helpful when treating OCD. Examples of herbs that may reduce anxiety and encourage relaxation are chamomile, passionflower, and valerian.

Safety Points To Remember

Herbal medicines are typically regarded as safe, but it's important to use caution when using them, particularly if you have mental health issues.

To be sure that herbal remedies don't worsen underlying medical disorders or interfere badly with any current prescriptions, it's best to speak with a healthcare provider.

 It is also important to talk about the right dosage and length of usage to optimize advantages and reduce hazards.

Selecting The Proper Herbs To Treat OCD

When choosing the appropriate herbs to manage OCD, it's important to take the individual's demands and symptoms into account.

Herbs with nervine, anxiolytic, and adaptogenic qualities might be useful. Herbs that are known for their calming properties include lavender, lemon balm, skullcap, and valerian in addition to chamomile, passionflower, and valerian.

A professional herbalist or healthcare professional can assist in customizing an herbal regimen to address each person's particular OCD symptoms.

It is essential to comprehend OCD, its symptoms, and its possible origins to create herbal remedies that work. Herbal treatments can be a part of a comprehensive strategy to manage OCD and support mental health when they are used carefully and in conjunction with professional assistance.

CHAPTER TWO

HERBS AND THEIR MEDICAL ADVANTAGES

Since ancient times, people from many different cultures have used herbs for their therapeutic qualities, which provide all-natural solutions for a variety of health issues.

Herbs are useful in the treatment of mental health issues such as obsessive-compulsive disorder (OCD). These plants frequently have substances that interact with the body's processes to enhance stability, relaxation, and cognitive performance.

Herbs That Calm Anxiety

Some herbs are particularly effective at reducing anxiety because of their ability to relax the nervous system. One such botanical with anxiolytic qualities is passionflower. Passionflower has a calming impact on people who are suffering from obsessive-compulsive disorders because of its interaction with neurotransmitters in the brain. Another herb that is well-known for calming nerves and lowering tension is chamomile. For people who are experiencing overpowering thoughts and routines related to obsessive-compulsive disorder (OCD), incorporating these relaxing herbs into one's routine may provide relief.

Mood-Releasing Herbs

Mood swings are a common feature of obsessive-compulsive disorder, and adding mood-stabilizing herbs to one's wellness routine can be quite beneficial. For example, research has been done on the possibility of St. John's Wort to help reduce symptoms of depression and improve mood stability. This herb helps promote a more stable emotional state by interacting with neurotransmitters such as serotonin. Furthermore, the adaptogenic herb Rhodiola rosea has been identified as having stress-relieving qualities, which may help people cope with the emotional difficulties that come with OCD.

Herbs For Mental Health

Improving cognitive function is an essential part of treating obsessive-compulsive disorder since it entails releasing recurrent patterns of thought and behavior. The ginkgo biloba plant, which is produced from its leaves, is well known for its ability to improve cognitive function.

This herb is said to promote cognitive functions including memory and focus by increasing blood flow to the brain. Studies on bacopa monnieri have revealed that it may have favorable effects on memory and general cognitive function, making it another herb that has attracted interest for its possible cognitive advantages.

Including these herbs in a complete approach could help make the mind more flexible and robust while dealing with OCD symptoms.

An investigation into the world of herbal remedies for OCD symptoms uncovers a wide range of plants with potential benefits.

The vast field of herbal treatments offers a wealth of possibilities for those looking for natural alternatives.

These include mood-stabilizing, cognitive-boosting, and relaxing plants that relieve anxiety. Before adding new herbs to one's regimen, as with any health-related undertaking, it is best to speak with medical professionals, particularly for individuals who are managing complicated disorders like OCD.

CHAPTER THREE

HERBAL TREATMENTS FOR ANXIOUS THOUGHT

The mental health disorder known as Obsessive-Compulsive Disorder (OCD), which is typified by recurring intrusive thoughts and repetitive actions, can be difficult to control. While there are standard treatments like counseling and medicine, some people look for supplementary methods like herbal cures. This article examines several herbal remedies that could lessen OCD-related compulsive thinking.

Making Herbal Concoctions

For millennia, people have utilized herbal infusions—often in the form of teas or extracts—to support mental health. For example, chamomile is well known for its relaxing effects.

Chamomile tea has the potential to alleviate anxiety and encourage relaxation, making it a viable option for those who are experiencing obsessive thoughts. Similarly, plants with relaxing properties like lemon balm and passionflower could be useful friends in treating OCD symptoms.

Aromatherapy Using Essential Oils

Aromatherapy is a complementary treatment for mental health issues that uses essential oils to improve both physical and psychological well-being. It is becoming more and more popular.

It is thought that essential oils with calming properties, such as frankincense, bergamot, and lavender, can help calm the mind.

Incorporating these oils into aromatherapy sessions may provide a soothing environment, potentially assisting individuals dealing with obsessive thoughts.

Whether diffused in the air or applied topically with a carrier oil, essential oils can be a valuable addition to a holistic OCD management plan.

Herbal Teas And Tinctures

Herbal teas and tinctures offer another avenue for individuals seeking natural remedies for obsessive thoughts.

Valerian root, known for its sedative properties, is a common ingredient in herbal teas that may promote relaxation and calmness.

Skullcap and holy basil are herbs that have been traditionally used to support the nervous system, and incorporating them into tinctures may offer a gentle approach to managing obsessive-compulsive symptoms.

It's crucial to approach herbal remedies with caution and consult with a healthcare professional before incorporating them into an OCD management plan.

While these herbal solutions may provide additional support, they are not a substitute for evidence-based treatments.

Integrating herbal remedies with traditional therapeutic approaches may offer a comprehensive strategy for individuals navigating the challenges of obsessive-compulsive disorders.

CHAPTER FOUR

LIFESTYLE CHANGES FOR OCD MANAGEMENT

Living with obsessive-compulsive disorder (OCD) can be challenging, but incorporating certain lifestyle changes can significantly contribute to its management. Embracing a holistic approach that goes beyond medication, these changes focus on various aspects of daily life to alleviate symptoms and improve overall well-being.

Nutrition And Dietary Considerations

Diet plays a crucial role in mental health, and for individuals dealing with OCD, certain nutritional choices may positively impact their condition. While there's no specific "OCD diet," maintaining a balanced and nutritious eating plan can support overall mental health. Including foods rich in omega-3 fatty acids, antioxidants, and vitamins may contribute to better brain function and potentially help manage OCD symptoms.

Exercise And Physical Activity

Regular physical activity is not only beneficial for physical health but can also play a significant role in managing OCD. Engaging in exercises like aerobic activities, yoga, or even simple daily walks can help reduce anxiety and stress levels, common triggers for OCD symptoms. Exercise releases endorphins, the body's natural mood enhancers, which can contribute to an improved mental state.

Stress-Reduction Techniques

Stress is often a key factor in triggering OCD symptoms, and adopting stress-reduction techniques can be instrumental in managing the condition

Practices such as mindfulness meditation, deep breathing exercises, and progressive muscle relaxation can help individuals with OCD gain better control over their thoughts and reduce overall stress levels. These techniques promote relaxation and can be integrated into daily routines for long-term benefits.

By incorporating these lifestyle changes into their daily lives, individuals with OCD can create a supportive environment that complements other therapeutic approaches.

While these lifestyle adjustments may not replace professional treatment, they can serve as valuable tools in the comprehensive management of obsessive-compulsive disorder.

CHAPTER FIVE

CASE STUDIES

Obsessive-Compulsive Disorder (OCD) is a mental health condition characterized by persistent, unwanted thoughts (obsessions) and repetitive behaviors or mental acts (compulsions). Exploring case studies can provide valuable insights into the diverse ways individuals experience and manage OCD. These case studies often showcase the unique challenges people face and the effectiveness of herbal solutions in their journeys toward recovery.

Real-Life Experiences

Understanding OCD from a real-life perspective involves delving into the daily experiences of individuals grappling with this disorder.

Real-life experiences offer a nuanced look at how OCD impacts various aspects of a person's life, including relationships, work, and overall well-being.

Examining these experiences sheds light on the multifaceted nature of OCD and the potential benefits of herbal remedies in mitigating its symptoms.

Successful Herbal Approaches

Herbal solutions have gained attention for their potential in managing OCD symptoms. Examining success stories and documented instances of individuals finding relief through herbal approaches provides hope and inspiration.

This section explores different herbal remedies and their positive impact on individuals with OCD. From traditional herbs to modern adaptations, the focus is on showcasing the diversity of successful herbal approaches in the treatment of obsessive-compulsive disorder.

In delving into case studies, readers can gain a deeper understanding of the complexities surrounding OCD.

Real-life experiences offer a human touch to the clinical understanding of the disorder, fostering empathy and awareness. Finally, exploring successful herbal approaches highlights the potential of alternative remedies in providing relief for those affected by OCD.

CHAPTER SIX

GUIDELINES FOR USING HERBAL SOLUTIONS

When considering herbal solutions for OCD, it is crucial to approach them with caution and under the guidance of a healthcare professional. Herbal remedies can interact with medications and may not be suitable for everyone.

Before incorporating herbs into your treatment plan, consult with a qualified healthcare provider to ensure they are safe and effective for your specific situation.

Dosage And Administration

Proper dosage and administration are key factors in maximizing the benefits of herbal solutions for OCD. The recommended dosage can vary based on the specific herb and individual factors such as age, weight, and overall health.

It is essential to follow the dosage guidelines provided by healthcare professionals or herbalists. Additionally, herbal supplements should be taken consistently as directed for optimal results.

Potential Interactions

Interactions between herbal remedies and conventional medications are a critical consideration.

Certain herbs may interfere with the effectiveness of prescribed medications or exacerbate side effects.

It is imperative to inform your healthcare provider about any herbal supplements you are taking to prevent potential interactions.

Regular communication with your healthcare team helps ensure a comprehensive and safe treatment approach.

Monitoring Progress

Monitoring progress is essential when using herbal solutions for OCD. Keep track of changes in symptoms, mood, and overall well-being. Regular check-ins with your healthcare provider can help assess the effectiveness of herbal remedies and make necessary adjustments to your treatment plan. If there are any concerns or unexpected changes, it is crucial to communicate openly with your healthcare team for appropriate guidance.

In conclusion, herbal solutions for OCD can be a complementary approach to conventional treatments. However, it is vital to approach them with mindfulness, following guidelines for usage, paying attention to dosage, being aware of potential interactions, and consistently monitoring progress. Always consult with healthcare professionals to ensure a holistic and personalized treatment plan that addresses your unique needs.

CHAPTER SEVEN

INCORPORATING HERBAL SOLUTIONS INTO DAILY LIFE

Understanding how to integrate herbal solutions into daily life is a crucial aspect of managing OCD. This section explores various herbs and their potential benefits, offering practical guidance on dosage, preparation methods, and possible side effects. By incorporating herbs into daily routines, individuals may find a supportive and natural means of managing their symptoms.

Developing A Routine

Establishing a consistent routine is essential for individuals managing OCD. This chapter delves into the significance of routines in promoting mental well-being and explores how herbal solutions can be seamlessly integrated into daily practices. From morning rituals to evening routines, readers will discover practical ways to make herbs a sustainable and accessible part of their daily lives.

Long-Term Strategies

Managing OCD requires a comprehensive and long-term approach. This section explores strategies for incorporating herbal solutions as part of a sustained mental health plan.

Readers will gain insights into the importance of consistency and adaptability, recognizing that herbal remedies may contribute to long-term well-being when integrated thoughtfully into one's lifestyle.

Combining Herbal And Traditional Approaches

While herbal solutions offer a natural alternative, they can also complement traditional approaches to OCD treatment.

This chapter explores the synergy between herbal remedies and conventional therapies, emphasizing the importance of a collaborative and holistic approach. By combining these two modalities, individuals may find a personalized and effective strategy for managing their obsessive-compulsive symptoms.

this book serves as a guide for individuals seeking to explore herbal solutions for obsessive-compulsive disorders.

 By understanding the principles behind herbal remedies and incorporating them into daily life, readers may discover additional tools to enhance their mental health journey.

It is essential to approach these solutions with an informed perspective, considering individual differences and consulting with healthcare professionals when needed.

CHAPTER EIGHT

HERBS FOR MOOD STABILIZATION:

Mood stabilization is a crucial aspect of managing OCD symptoms. This section explores different herbs renowned for their potential to positively influence mood and emotional well-being. By incorporating these herbs into one's lifestyle, individuals with OCD may find additional support in their journey toward mental health.

St. John's Wort:

St. John's Wort, scientifically known as Hypericum perforatum, is a well-known herb with a history of traditional use for mood disorders. Studies suggest that it may have antidepressant properties and could be beneficial for individuals dealing with OCD. The active compounds in St. John's Wort are believed to impact neurotransmitters in the brain, potentially contributing to mood stabilization.

Rhodiola:

Rhodiola, also referred to as Rhodiola rosea, is an adaptogenic herb known for its stress-relieving properties.

Adaptogens are substances that may help the body adapt to stressors, both physical and emotional.

 Rhodiola is thought to modulate the body's stress response, potentially aiding individuals in managing the anxiety and stress associated with OCD.

Ashwagandha:

Ashwagandha, scientifically named Withania somnifera, is an ancient herb with a rich history in traditional Ayurvedic medicine.

It is recognized for its adaptogenic qualities, helping the body cope with stress and anxiety. As OCD often involves heightened stress levels, incorporating ashwagandha into one's routine may contribute to a sense of calm and balance.

Ginkgo Biloba:

Ginkgo biloba, derived from the leaves of the ginkgo tree, is known for its potential cognitive benefits.

While its primary reputation lies in enhancing memory and cognitive function, some studies suggest that Ginkgo biloba may also have positive effects on mood.

Exploring the use of this herb could offer individuals with OCD an additional avenue for mood stabilization.

By understanding and incorporating these herbs into a comprehensive approach to mental health, individuals with OCD may find complementary support in managing their symptoms.

 It is important to consult with healthcare professionals before making significant changes to one's treatment plan and to ensure that herbal remedies do not interact negatively with prescribed medications.

This book serves as a guide for those seeking natural, herbal solutions to enhance their overall well-being while navigating the complexities of Obsessive-Compulsive Disorder.

CHAPTER NINE

HERBS FOR COGNITIVE FUNCTION

Cognitive function plays a crucial role in managing OCD symptoms, and certain herbs have been studied for their potential to support mental clarity and focus. The following herbs are explored in detail for their cognitive-enhancing properties.

Gotu Kola

Gotu Kola (Centella Asiatica) is a herb traditionally used in Ayurvedic medicine to enhance cognitive function. It contains compounds known as triterpenoids that may have neuroprotective effects. Gotu Kola is believed to support mental clarity and reduce anxiety, making it a potentially valuable herb for individuals with OCD seeking natural remedies.

Bacopa

Bacopa monnieri, commonly known as Bacopa, is a herb with a long history of use in traditional medicine. It is renowned for its potential to improve memory and cognitive function. Bacopa contains compounds called bacosides, which may contribute to its neuroprotective effects.

Exploring the use of Bacopa in managing OCD involves understanding how it interacts with the brain's neurotransmitters and cognitive processes.

Ginseng

Ginseng, particularly Panax ginseng, has been studied for its adaptogenic properties, which may help the body respond to stress.

As stress often exacerbates OCD symptoms, incorporating ginseng into a holistic approach may offer benefits.

Ginsenosides, the active compounds in ginseng, are believed to modulate various neurotransmitters and have potential cognitive-enhancing effects.

Rosemary

Rosemary (Rosmarinus officinalis) is an aromatic herb that has been traditionally used to improve memory and concentration. It contains compounds such as rosmarinic acid and 1,8-cineole, which may have neuroprotective and anti-inflammatory properties. Exploring the role of rosemary in managing OCD involves understanding how these compounds may positively influence cognitive function and potentially alleviate symptoms.

this guide provides valuable insights into herbal solutions for obsessive-compulsive disorders, focusing on herbs known for their cognitive-enhancing properties. Understanding the potential benefits of herbs like Gotu Kola, Bacopa, Ginseng, and Rosemary can empower individuals to explore natural remedies as part of their holistic approach to managing OCD symptoms.

CHAPTER TEN

INTEGRATING HERBAL SOLUTIONS WITH TRADITIONAL APPROACHES

Herbal solutions can be complementary to traditional OCD treatments. Certain herbs are known for their calming and anxiety-reducing properties, which can help alleviate some of the symptoms associated with OCD.

For example, herbs like chamomile and passionflower have natural sedative effects that may contribute to a sense of relaxation, potentially easing the anxiety linked to obsessive thoughts.

Additionally, adaptogenic herbs like ashwagandha and rhodiola can be incorporated into a comprehensive treatment plan.

These herbs are believed to help the body adapt to stress, which is often a significant trigger for individuals with OCD. Integrating these herbs may provide a more well-rounded approach to managing the psychological and physiological aspects of the disorder.

Collaboration With Healthcare Providers

It is crucial for individuals considering herbal solutions for OCD to collaborate closely with their healthcare providers.

Healthcare professionals, including psychiatrists, psychologists, and herbalists, can work together to create a customized treatment plan that addresses the unique needs of each individual. Open communication is key to ensuring that herbal remedies do not interfere with prescribed medications or exacerbate existing health conditions.

Moreover, healthcare providers can offer guidance on the appropriate dosage and potential side effects of herbal supplements. Regular check-ins with a mental health professional can help monitor progress and make adjustments to the treatment plan as needed. This collaborative approach ensures a comprehensive and well-monitored strategy for managing OCD.

Monitoring Progress

Monitoring progress is an essential aspect of incorporating herbal solutions into the treatment of OCD. Individuals should keep track of changes in symptoms, both positive and negative, and report these to their healthcare providers.

This collaborative monitoring allows for timely adjustments to the herbal regimen or other aspects of the treatment plan.

It's essential to recognize that herbal remedies may take time to show noticeable effects, and individual responses can vary. Patience is key, and a consistent approach to herbal supplementation, combined with traditional treatments, can contribute to long-term improvements. Regular evaluations with healthcare providers help assess the effectiveness of the chosen herbal solutions and make informed decisions about their continuation or modification.

In conclusion, the integration of herbal solutions with traditional approaches offers a promising avenue for managing obsessive-compulsive disorder.

Through collaboration with healthcare providers and diligent progress monitoring, individuals can explore the potential benefits of herbal remedies as part of a comprehensive and personalized treatment plan for OCD.

FINAL VERDICT

In wrapping up this exploration of herbal solutions for obsessive-compulsive disorders, the conclusion provides a summary of key findings. It reiterates the potential benefits of incorporating herbs into a comprehensive approach to managing OCD and encourages readers to explore these natural alternatives with an open mind.

Recap Of Key Points

To reinforce the essential information covered throughout the book, this section offers a concise recap of key points. Readers can use this recap as a quick reference guide, summarizing the core concepts and insights related to herbal solutions for obsessive-compulsive disorders.

Encouragement for Readers

Embarking on a journey to manage OCD through herbal solutions can be both empowering and challenging. This section provides words of encouragement, motivating readers to stay committed to their well-being and offer support for their exploration of herbal remedies. It emphasizes the importance of patience and consistency in integrating these natural approaches into one's lifestyle.

Resources For Further Exploration

to delve deeper into the world of herbal solutions for mental health, this section provides a curated list of resources. From books and websites to reputable practitioners, individuals can find additional information and guidance to enhance their understanding and implementation of herbal remedies for obsessive-compulsive disorders.